contents

NZ, Canada, US and UK readers
Please note that Australian cup and spoon
measurements are metric. A quick conversion
guide appears on page 63.

2 indian essential ingredients

By familiarising yourself with these important ingredients, and their correct usage, the brilliant recipes in this book will be easily mastered.

cardamom

Cardamom is the dried fruit of a perennial herb belonging to the ginger family, and is one of the most expensive spices in the world. Used in different forms – the pods are used to lend flavour during cooking, but removed prior to serving; the small seeds found within the pod are used either whole or ground, and are consumed – cardamom lends a warm, pungent taste and aroma to Indian cooking.

curry leaves

These shiny green leaves originate from a small tree that forms part of the wider citrus family. Curry leaves have a pleasant fragrance and are used as a flavouring in many curries and chutneys. They are available dried and fresh; whole leaves are usually removed from a cooked dish before serving.

ground cardamom

cardamom seeds

cardamom pods

black cardamom pods

garam masala

Masala means spice mixture in India, and mixtures such as garam masala are the essence of Indian cookery. Usually including various proportions of cinnamon, cloves, black pepper and cardamom, garam masala may also contain coriander and cumin, and occasionally even fennel and cassia. The spices of garam masala are ground and dry-roasted before being added to a dish. As the mix is highly fragrant, it should be used sparingly.

curry leaves

coconut cream and milk

Coconut cream is a sweet, thick liquid produced by soaking grated fresh coconut in boiling water, allowing it to cool, then squeezing the liquid from the pulp through a muslin cloth or equivalent. Completing the process again, with the same grated coconut, results in coconut milk, a thinner but still fragrant liquid.

ghee

Ghee is clarified and evaporated butter – melted butter simmered just long enough to boil off its water content. Nutty tasting, ghee is usually used as a cooking medium for meat, and is an essential ingredient in many Indian recipes.

basmati rice

This variety of white rice is long-grained, and has a subtly aromatic flavour. Basmati rice grains stay separate when they are cooked, making it a rice perfectly suited to pilaf and other fragrant rice dishes that are an important part of Indian cooking.

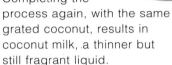

black mustard seeds

Black mustard seeds are the seed of a plant from the cabbage family. In Indian cookery, these seeds are fried whole before being added to dishes – this application of heat creates a mild nutty flavour, rather than the sharp flavour usually associated with mustard.

black mustard seeds

ginger

The root-like, subterranean stem of a plant, ginger is commonly used in Indian cooking. Ginger lends a delicious pungency to recipes and, though used fresh in Indian dishes, ginger is also available dried, pickled or ground. It is important to note that dried, pickled or ground ginger is no substitute where a recipe calls for fresh ginger.

ginger

4 curried cream of carrot soup

60g butter

1 medium leek (350g), chopped coarsely

2 cloves garlic, crushed

2 teaspoons garam masala

2 teaspoons ground cumin

1/3 cup (90g) mild curry paste

3 large carrots (540g), chopped coarsely

2 large parsnips (360g), chopped coarsely

1.75 litres (7 cups) chicken stock

2 tablespoons tomato paste

1/2 cup (125ml) coconut milk

Melt butter in large saucepan; cook leek, garlic, spices and curry paste, stirring, about 5 minutes or until leek is soft. Add carrot, parsnip and stock; simmer, covered, about 30 minutes or until vegetables are very soft. Stir in tomato paste. Blend or process mixture, in batches, until smooth; return soup to pan, stir until hot. Serve soup drizzled with coconut milk.

SERVES 4
Per serving 28.5g fat; 1684kJ

1 tablespoon
vegetable oil

1 medium brown
onion (150g),
chopped coarsely

2 cloves garlic,
crushed

¼ cup (65g) mild
curry paste

1 large apple (200g)

1 medium carrot
(120g), chopped
coarsely

1 medium potato
(200g), chopped
coarsely

½ cup (100g)
red lentils

1 litre (4 cups)
chicken stock

1 tablespoon
lemon juice

½ cup (65g) coconut
milk powder

1 cup (250ml) water

8 pappadums

vegetable oil,
for deep-frying

¼ cup (70g) yogurt

Heat oil in large saucepan; cook onion and garlic, stirring, until onion is soft. Add paste; cook, stirring, until fragrant. Coarsely grate enough peeled cored apple to make 2 tablespoons; reserve. Coarsely chop remaining apple; add to pan with carrot, potato, lentils and stock. Bring to a boil; reduce heat, simmer, covered, about 15 minutes or until lentils and vegetables are tender.
Blend or process mixture, in batches, until pureed. Return soup to pan, add juice and blended coconut milk powder and the water; stir until hot.
Meanwhile, deep-fry pappadums in hot oil until puffed and crisp; drain on absorbent paper. Serve soup, sprinkled with reserved apple and drizzled with yogurt, with pappadums.

SERVES 4
Per serving 25g fat; 1719kJ

6 pumpkin, lentil

and herb curry

2 tablespoons vegetable oil

2 medium brown onions (300g),
chopped finely

2 cloves garlic, crushed

1 tablespoon finely chopped
fresh thyme leaves

3 teaspoons vindaloo paste

1.2kg pumpkin, chopped coarsely

1 large potato (300g), chopped coarsely

2 small tomatoes (260g), chopped coarsely

2 cups (500ml) vegetable stock

1 1/2 cups (375ml) water

1/4 cup (60g) tomato paste

1/2 cup (100g) red lentils

1 tablespoon finely chopped fresh
coriander leaves

1 tablespoon finely chopped fresh
flat-leaf parsley

Heat oil in large saucepan; cook onion,
garlic, thyme and curry paste, stirring, until
onion is soft. Add pumpkin, potato, tomato,
stock, the water, tomato paste and lentils;
simmer, covered, about 15 minutes or until
vegetables and lentils are tender. Stir in herbs.
Serve with green salad, if desired.

SERVES 4
Per serving 12.8g fat; 1502kJ

8 raan

1 teaspoon ground cumin

1 teaspoon ground cardamom

1 teaspoon ground coriander

1/4 teaspoon ground clove

1/4 teaspoon ground cinnamon

1/2 teaspoon chilli powder

1/2 teaspoon cracked black pepper

3 cloves garlic, crushed

1 tablespoon grated fresh ginger

2 tablespoons tomato paste

1/4 cup (60ml) lemon juice

4 (1kg) mini lamb roasts

2 cups (500ml) boiling water

Combine spices in small dry saucepan; cook, stirring, until fragrant. Combine spices in small bowl with garlic, ginger, paste and juice. Pierce lamb all over with sharp knife. Rub spice mixture all over lamb, pressing firmly into cuts. Place lamb in large bowl, cover; refrigerate overnight.

Pour the water into large baking dish; place lamb on wire rack in dish. Bake, uncovered, in hot oven about 40 minutes or until browned and cooked as desired. Stand, covered, 10 minutes.

Serve with chapatis and tomato salad, if desired.

SERVES 4

Per serving 14.7g fat; 1469kJ

10 coconut pilaf

1 tablespoon
flaked coconut

2 cups (400g) basmati
rice, washed, drained

400ml coconut milk

1³/₄ cups (430ml) water

pinch saffron powder

¹/₄ cup (40g) raisins

1 teaspoon peanut oil

1 teaspoon cumin seeds

1 tablespoon
sesame seeds

¹/₄ cup (35g) unsalted
raw cashews

Cook coconut over medium heat in small frying pan, stirring, until lightly browned. Remove from pan, cool.

Combine rice, coconut milk, the water and saffron in large saucepan; stir over high heat until mixture boils. Add raisins; simmer, partly covered, 5 minutes or until most of the liquid is absorbed. Cover, cook over very low heat 5 minutes. Remove from heat; leave covered in pan. Heat oil in small frying pan; cook seeds and nuts over medium heat, stirring, until lightly browned. Stir into rice. Sprinkle hot rice with toasted coconut to serve.

SERVES 6
Per serving 12.2g fat; 1603kJ

1½ cups (225g) plain flour

1 tablespoon peanut oil

¼ cup (60ml) water

2 large potatoes (300g), chopped finely

¾ cup (90g) frozen peas, thawed

1 teaspoon ground cumin

½ teaspoon chilli powder

½ teaspoon ground cinnamon

2 tablespoons currants

1 tablespoon chopped fresh coriander leaves

2 tablespoons lemon juice

1 tablespoon soy sauce

vegetable oil, for deep-frying

Place flour in medium bowl, gradually stir in oil and the water; mix to a firm dough, knead on floured surface until smooth. Cover pastry; refrigerate 1 hour.
Boil, steam or microwave potato until tender; drain, cool. Combine potato, peas, cumin, chilli and cinnamon in large bowl. Stir in currants, coriander, juice and sauce.
Roll out half the pastry, on floured surface, to form 30cm x 40cm rectangle. Cut pastry into rounds using 10cm cutter. Place a heaped tablespoon of potato mixture on half of each round. Fold rounds in half, pressing edges together with a fork. Repeat with remaining pastry and potato mixture. Deep-fry batches of pastries in hot oil until golden brown; drain on absorbent paper. Serve hot.

MAKES 24
Per pastry 2.8g fat; 293kJ

12 aloo tikka

1/3 cup (85g) yellow split peas

3 large potatoes (900g), chopped coarsely

1/2 cup (75g) chickpea flour

1 tablespoon finely chopped fresh mint leaves

1 tablespoon finely chopped fresh coriander leaves

2 teaspoons garam masala

1 teaspoon ground cumin

1 teaspoon ground coriander

2 red thai chillies, chopped finely

1 egg yolk

1 tablespoon lemon juice

1 teaspoon salt

chickpea flour, extra

60g ghee

1 egg, beaten lightly

tamarind sauce

1 cup (250ml) boiling water

50g dried tamarind, chopped finely

2 teaspoons grated fresh ginger

1 teaspoon ground cumin

50g palm sugar, chopped finely

Place split peas in medium bowl, cover with water, stand 45 minutes; drain. Place split peas in medium saucepan, cover with cold water, bring to a boil; reduce heat, simmer, uncovered, about 10 minutes or until just tender. Drain.

Boil, steam or microwave potatoes until tender; drain, mash in large bowl. Cool.

Add flour, herbs, spices, chilli, egg yolk, juice and salt to mashed potato. Stir in split peas. Mould mixture into balls then flatten to form patties. Dust patties with extra flour, shake off excess.

Heat ghee in large non-stick frying pan; dip patties, one at a time, in egg. Cook patties, in batches, until browned both sides; drain on absorbent paper. Serve patties with Tamarind Sauce.

Tamarind Sauce Combine the water and tamarind in small bowl; stand 30 minutes. Strain tamarind into small saucepan, pressing pulp to extract all liquid; discard tamarind pulp. Add ginger, cumin and palm sugar to pan, bring to a boil; simmer, uncovered, about 5 minutes or until sauce thickens slightly. Strain sauce, serve warm.

SERVES 6
Per serving 13.6g fat; 1470kJ

14 seafood curry

with coriander and mint

500g thick white fish fillets

500g medium
uncooked prawns

500g small black mussels

2 tablespoons ghee

1 large brown onion
(200g), sliced thinly

3 cloves garlic, crushed

1 tablespoon grated
fresh ginger

1 red thai chilli, chopped finely

2 teaspoons ground coriander

2 teaspoons ground cumin

1 tablespoon sweet paprika

2 curry leaves, shredded finely

400g can tomatoes

1 cup (250ml) coconut milk

2 teaspoons brown sugar

1 tablespoon fresh
coriander leaves

1 tablespoon fresh mint leaves

Cut fish into 4cm pieces. Shell and devein prawns, leaving tails intact. Scrub mussels, remove beards.

Heat ghee in large saucepan; cook onion, garlic, ginger and chilli, stirring, until onion is soft and browned lightly.

Add spices and curry leaves; cook, stirring, until fragrant. Stir in undrained crushed tomatoes, coconut milk and sugar, bring to a boil; reduce heat, simmer, covered, 10 minutes.

Add seafood; simmer, covered, about 5 minutes or until fish and prawns have changed in colour and mussels have opened.

Gently stir in coriander and mint.

SERVES 4
Per serving 26.2g fat; 1968kJ

16 prawns with hot
lime pickle mayonnaise

20 large uncooked
prawns (1kg)

280g can
coconut milk

3 cloves garlic,
chopped coarsely

1 teaspoon mild
curry powder

1 teaspoon
sweet paprika

1 teaspoon
ground turmeric

1 teaspoon
ground cumin

1 tablespoon coarsely
chopped fresh
coriander leaves

3 red thai chillies,
chopped coarsely

hot lime pickle
mayonnaise

1 cup (300g)
mayonnaise

1/3 cup (80ml) bottled
hot lime pickle

2 tablespoons
coarsely chopped
fresh coriander leaves

1/2 cup (120g)
sour cream

Shell and devein prawns, leaving heads
and tails intact. Place prawns in large bowl.
Process remaining ingredients until smooth,
combine with prawns in bowl. Cover,
refrigerate 3 hours or overnight.
Drain prawns, discard marinade. Cook on
heated oiled grill plate (or grill or barbecue)
until browned lightly both sides and changed in
colour. Serve with Hot Lime Pickle Mayonnaise.
Hot Lime Pickle Mayonnaise Blend or process
ingredients until smooth. Cover, refrigerate
at least 1 hour.

SERVES 4
Per serving 46.2g fat; 2529kJ

1¹/₂ cups (300g) dried chickpeas

2 tablespoons vegetable oil

1 medium brown onion (150g), chopped finely

1 teaspoon grated fresh ginger

3 cloves garlic, crushed

2 teaspoons garam masala

2 teaspoons ground cumin

2 teaspoons ground coriander

2 teaspoons sweet paprika

¹/₂ teaspoon chilli powder

¹/₄ teaspoon ground turmeric

1 teaspoon yellow mustard seeds

400g can tomatoes

2 tablespoons coconut cream

1 teaspoon salt

Place chickpeas in medium bowl, cover with water, soak overnight, drain. Boil or microwave chickpeas in water, until tender; drain.

Heat oil in large frying pan; cook onion, stirring, until onion is lightly browned. Add ginger, garlic, spices and seeds; cook, stirring, until fragrant.

Add undrained crushed tomatoes, coconut cream, salt and chickpeas; cook, stirring, about 5 minutes or until mixture is thickened.

SERVES 4
Per serving 16g fat; 1391kJ

18 lamb, butter bean
and spinach curry

2 tablespoons ghee

500g diced lamb shoulder

2 medium brown onions
(300g), chopped finely

4 cloves garlic, crushed

2 teaspoons grated
fresh ginger

1 teaspoon cumin seeds

1 red thai chilli,
chopped finely

1 teaspoon garam masala

2 teaspoons ground cumin

2 teaspoons
ground coriander

1 teaspoon
ground turmeric

4 curry leaves, torn

1/2 cup (125ml)
tomato puree

1 cup (250ml) beef stock

3/4 cup (180ml) water

1/2 cup (125ml)
coconut cream

300g can butter beans,
rinsed, drained

100g baby spinach leaves

Heat ghee in large saucepan; cook lamb until browned all over, remove from pan. **Cook** onion, garlic, ginger, seeds and chilli, stirring, until onion is soft. Add ground spices and curry leaves; cook, stirring, until fragrant. **Return** lamb to pan with puree, stock, the water and coconut cream; simmer, covered, stirring occasionally, about 1 1/2 hours or until lamb is very tender. **Add** beans and spinach; cook until spinach is just beginning to wilt.

SERVES 4
Per serving
23.5g fat; 1576kJ

20 lamb rogan josh

Heat oil in large saucepan; cook lamb, in batches, until browned all over.

Add garlic, onion, chilli, ground spices, seeds and cinnamon to same pan; cook, stirring, until onion is soft. Return lamb to pan with tomato and puree, bring to a boil; reduce heat, simmer, covered, about 1 hour or until lamb is tender.

Just before serving, stir in whisked yogurt.

2 tablespoons peanut oil

800g diced lamb

4 cloves garlic, crushed

1 large red onion (300g), chopped finely

3 red thai chillies, chopped finely

2 teaspoons ground cumin

1 teaspoon ground cardamom

1 teaspoon ground clove

2 teaspoons ground ginger

1/4 cup (40g) poppy seeds

1 cinnamon stick

3 small tomatoes (400g), chopped coarsely

400g can tomato puree

1 cup (280g) yogurt

SERVES 4
Per serving 23.9g fat; 2031kJ

coconut curried
vegetables

1 medium kumara
(400g), sliced thickly

1 small cauliflower
(1kg), chopped
coarsely

2 tablespoons ghee

2 teaspoons
ground cumin

1 teaspoon
ground coriander

1 teaspoon
garam masala

2 teaspoons
ground turmeric

1/2 teaspoon
sweet paprika

1 large brown onion
(200g), sliced thinly

2 cloves garlic,
crushed

2 medium carrots
(240g), sliced thinly

400g broccoli,
chopped coarsely

350g snake beans,
chopped coarsely

12/3 cups (400ml)
coconut cream

Boil, steam or microwave kumara and
cauliflower until just tender; drain. Heat ghee
in large frying pan; cook spices until fragrant.
Add onion and garlic; cook, stirring, until
onion is browned lightly.
Add carrot, broccoli and beans; cook,
stirring, until vegetables are just tender.
Add kumara, cauliflower and coconut cream;
cook, stirring, until sauce boils.

SERVES 4
Per serving 32.6g fat; 2078kJ

22 lamb kofta curry

750g minced lamb

1½ tablespoons
finely chopped fresh
mint leaves

¼ cup (70g) yogurt

½ teaspoon chilli powder

3 teaspoons
garam masala

3 teaspoons
ground cumin

1 teaspoon
ground turmeric

2 tablespoons
vegetable oil

1 large brown onion
(200g), chopped finely

2 teaspoons
grated fresh ginger

1 clove garlic, crushed

2 tablespoons
yogurt, extra

2 tablespoons
almond meal

400g can tomatoes

1 cup (250ml)
chicken stock

1 tablespoon finely
chopped fresh
coriander leaves

Combine lamb, mint, yogurt and 3 teaspoons of the combined ground spices in large bowl. Shape rounded tablespoons of mixture into kofta. Heat half of the oil in large non-stick frying pan; cook kofta, in batches, until browned all over, drain on absorbent paper. **Heat** remaining oil in same pan; cook onion, ginger and garlic, stirring, until onion is soft. **Add** remaining ground spices; cook, stirring, until fragrant. Add extra yogurt gradually, in four batches, stirring between additions. Stir in almond meal, undrained crushed tomatoes and stock, bring to a boil; reduce heat, simmer, uncovered, about 10 minutes or until thickened slightly.

Add kofta to pan; simmer, uncovered, about 15 minutes or until kofta are cooked through and sauce has thickened. Stir in coriander.

SERVES 4
Per serving 31.7g fat; 2075kJ

24 tandoori chicken
wings

400g can
tomato puree

1 clove garlic, crushed

2 teaspoons
sambal oelek

2 teaspoons
sweet paprika

2 teaspoons
garam masala

2 teaspoons
ground coriander

2 teaspoons
ground cumin

2 tablespoons yogurt

12 large chicken
wings (1.5kg)

cucumber raita

1 Lebanese
cucumber (130g)

3/4 cup (210g) yogurt

Combine ingredients in large bowl. Cover, refrigerate 3 hours or overnight.
Drain chicken, discard marinade. Cook on heated oiled grill plate
(or grill or barbecue) until browned both sides and cooked through.
Serve with Cucumber Raita.
Cucumber Raita Cut cucumber in half lengthways, remove seeds with
a teaspoon; chop cucumber finely. Combine cucumber and yogurt
in small bowl.

MAKES 12
Per serving 3g fat; 359kJ

1 cup (280g) yogurt

1 medium brown
onion (150g),
chopped coarsely

2 tablespoons
lemon juice

1 tablespoon
vegetable oil

1 tablespoon finely
chopped fresh ginger

3 cloves garlic,
chopped coarsely

2 teaspoons
chilli powder

1 teaspoon
garam masala

1 teaspoon
ground cumin

tiny pinch
tandoori powder

12 (780g) lamb cutlets

Blend or process yogurt, onion, juice, oil, ginger, garlic, spices and powder until pureed. Combine lamb cutlets with pureed yogurt mixture in large bowl; cover, refrigerate overnight.

Drain lamb, discard marinade. Cook on heated oiled grill plate (or grill or barbecue) until browned both sides and cooked as desired.

SERVES 4
Per serving 16.3g fat; 1177kJ

26 pork vindaloo

1kg diced pork

1 tablespoon vegetable oil

2 large brown onions (400g), sliced thinly

1 cup vegetable stock

vindaloo paste

2 teaspoons ground cumin

1 teaspoon chilli powder

2 teaspoons black mustard seeds

1 1/2 teaspoons ground cinnamon

1/3 cup (80ml) white wine vinegar

1 teaspoon salt

1 teaspoon sugar

1 teaspoon ground cardamom

2 teaspoons ground turmeric

1/2 teaspoon ground clove

1 teaspoon cracked black pepper

3 cloves garlic, crushed

1 1/2 teaspoons ground ginger

mango sambal

1 medium mango (430g), chopped finely

1 red thai chilli, chopped finely

1 tablespoon lemon juice

1 tablespoon finely chopped fresh mint leaves

Cut pork into 3cm pieces. Heat oil in large saucepan; cook pork, in batches, until browned all over.
Cook onion in same pan, stirring, until soft. Add Vindaloo Paste; cook, stirring, until fragrant. Add stock, return pork to pan; bring to a boil. Reduce heat; simmer, uncovered, over low heat, stirring occasionally, about 1 hour or until pork is tender. Serve with Mango Sambal.
Vindaloo Paste Combine ingredients in small bowl, stand 30 minutes before using.
Mango Sambal Combine ingredients in small bowl; cover, refrigerate at least 1 hour.

SERVES 4
Per serving 15.2g fat; 1863kJ

28 lamb korma

1 tablespoon
peanut oil

1 red thai chilli,
chopped finely

2 large brown onions
(400g), sliced thinly

3 cloves
garlic, crushed

2 tablespoons grated
fresh ginger

1 tablespoon
ground cumin

3 teaspoons
ground coriander

1½ teaspoons
garam masala

1.5kg diced lamb

1⅔ cups (400ml)
coconut milk

¾ cup (210g) yogurt

400g can tomatoes

6 cardamom
pods, bruised

1 cinnamon stick

⅓ cup (25g) flaked
almonds, toasted

1 tablespoon
tamarind concentrate

Heat oil in large saucepan; cook chilli, onion, garlic, ginger and ground spices, stirring, until onion is soft. Stir lamb into spice mixture; add combined coconut milk and yogurt gradually, stirring well between each addition.

Add undrained crushed tomatoes, pods and cinnamon, bring to a boil; reduce heat, simmer, covered, 1 hour. Remove lid; simmer, stirring occasionally, about 1 hour or until lamb is tender. Just before serving, stir in almonds and tamarind.

SERVES 4
Per serving 45.1g fat; 3476kJ

crunchy spiced
potato wedges

5 medium
potatoes (1kg)

60g ghee, melted

2 cloves
garlic, crushed

1 teaspoon grated
fresh ginger

2 teaspoons black
mustard seeds

2 teaspoons
garam masala

2 teaspoons
ground cumin

1/4 teaspoon
chilli powder

1/2 teaspoon cracked
black pepper

1/2 teaspoon salt

Peel then halve each potato, cut each half into three wedges. Combine potatoes with remaining ingredients in large bowl.
Place potato mixture into large non-stick baking dish. Bake, uncovered, in very hot oven, turning occasionally, about 15 minutes or until browned all over and tender.

SERVES 4
Per serving 15.7g fat; 1281kJ

barbecued chicken
tikka kebabs

*Soak bamboo skewers in water for
at least 1 hour before using to prevent
them scorching.*

*1 medium brown onion (150g),
chopped coarsely*

2 cloves garlic, chopped coarsely

1/2 cup (135g) tikka paste

1/2 cup (140g) yogurt

1kg chicken thigh fillets, chopped coarsely

*1 tablespoon finely chopped
fresh coriander leaves*

1/2 cup (175g) mango chutney

*1 tablespoon finely chopped
fresh mint leaves*

Blend or process onion, garlic, paste
and yogurt until smooth. Combine pureed
yogurt mixture with chicken and coriander
in large bowl. Cover; refrigerate 3 hours
or overnight.
Drain chicken over medium bowl; reserve
marinade. Thread chicken onto 12 skewers.
Barbecue (or grill or char-grill) kebabs
until browned all over and cooked
through, brushing with reserved marinade
occasionally during cooking. Serve
with combined chutney and mint.

SERVES 4
Per serving 29.7g fat; 2440kJ

Put out the fire in your mouth (or fuel it further) with these delicious accompaniments to many a curry.

fresh mango and chilli relish

2 medium mangoes (860g), chopped finely

1 red thai chilli, chopped finely

1 teaspoon grated fresh ginger

1 tablespoon finely chopped fresh coriander leaves

Combine ingredients in medium bowl. Serve immediately.

Serves 8
(MAKES 2$\frac{1}{2}$ CUPS)
per tbsp 0.3g fat; 48kJ

tomato and mint sambal

1 teaspoon cumin seeds

3 medium tomatoes (570g), seeded, chopped finely

2 green onions, chopped finely

2 tablespoons finely shredded fresh mint leaves

1 tablespoon lime juice

1 teaspoon sugar

$\frac{1}{2}$ teaspoon salt

Cook seeds in small dry saucepan, stirring, until fragrant. Combine tomato with seeds and remaining ingredients in medium bowl. Serve immediately.

Serves 6
(MAKES 1$\frac{1}{2}$ CUPS)
per tbsp 0g fat; 8kJ

fresh mango and chilli relish

tomato and mint sambal

fresh mint and chilli sambal

This recipe is very spicy – serve only in small quantities.

1 cup firmly packed fresh mint leaves

4 green onions, chopped coarsely

1 red thai chilli, chopped coarsely

1 clove garlic, chopped coarsely

1 teaspoon cumin seeds

1/2 teaspoon salt

2 teaspoons sugar

2 tablespoons lime juice

1 tablespoon water

Blend or process ingredients until smooth. Transfer mixture to small bowl, cover surface tightly with plastic wrap; refrigerate at least 30 minutes.

Serves 6
(MAKES 1/2 CUP)
per tbsp 0.1g fat; 52kJ

cucumber and yogurt raita

1 teaspoon cumin seeds

2 lebanese cucumbers (260g)

1 cup (280g) yogurt

2 tablespoons finely shredded fresh mint leaves

pinch cayenne pepper

Cook seeds in small dry saucepan, stirring, until fragrant. Cut cucumbers in half lengthways, remove seeds with a teaspoon. Chop cucumber coarsely. Combine cucumber with cumin seeds, yogurt and mint in medium bowl. Serve sprinkled with pepper.

Serves 8
(MAKES 2 CUPS)
per tbsp 0.4g fat; 39kJ

fresh mint and chilli sambal

cucumber and yogurt raita

34 lamb do piazza

5 cloves garlic,
chopped coarsely

2 teaspoons grated
fresh ginger

1 teaspoon
cardamom seeds

1 teaspoon
ground turmeric

1 teaspoon
cayenne pepper

2 tablespoons water

5 large brown onions
(1kg), sliced thinly

1kg diced lamb

1/3 cup (80ml)
vegetable oil

1 teaspoon
fennel seeds

2 teaspoons
fenugreek seeds

3/4 cup (210g) yogurt

4 small tomatoes
(500g), seeded,
chopped finely

2 cups (500ml)
beef stock

2 tablespoons
lime juice

1/4 cup finely chopped
fresh coriander leaves

Blend or process garlic, ginger, cardamom, turmeric, pepper, the water and half the onion until pureed; transfer marinade to large bowl.
Add lamb; toss to coat with marinade. Cover, refrigerate 3 hours or overnight.
Heat oil in large saucepan; cook remaining onion until browned lightly. Remove from pan; reserve. Add seeds to same pan; cook, stirring, until seeds pop. Add the lamb mixture; cook, stirring, until browned all over. Add yogurt, in four batches, stirring well between each addition. Add tomato and stock, bring to a boil; reduce heat, simmer, covered, about 1 hour or until lamb is tender. Add reserved onions; stir until hot.
Just before serving, stir in juice and coriander.

SERVES 4
Per serving 30.2g fat; 2519kJ

lamb pilaf

600g lamb fillets

¹/₄ cup (65g) mild curry paste

¹/₄ cup (60ml) vegetable oil

2 medium brown onions (300g), sliced thinly

1 teaspoon black mustard seeds

1 teaspoon ground turmeric

1 cup (200g) basmati rice

1¹/₄ cups (310ml) water

¹/₃ cup (55g) sultanas

³/₄ cup (120g) blanched almonds, toasted

2 tablespoons finely chopped fresh coriander leaves

Place lamb fillets in large bowl, coat with half the paste, cover; refrigerate 3 hours or overnight.

Heat 1 tablespoon of the oil in large saucepan; cook lamb, until browned all over and cooked as desired. Slice lamb thinly.

Heat remaining oil in same pan; cook onion, remaining paste, seeds and turmeric, stirring, until onion is soft. Add rice; cook, stirring, 2 minutes. Add the water, bring to a boil; reduce heat, simmer, covered, 12 minutes. Remove from heat, stand, covered, 5 minutes. Stir in lamb, sultanas, almonds and coriander.

SERVES 4
Per serving 41.4g fat; 3219kJ

char-grilled
masala
fish cutlets

4 (1kg) white fish cutlets

2 tablespoons ghee

masala marinade

1 cup loosely packed fresh
coriander leaves

4 cloves garlic, chopped coarsely

1 tablespoon finely chopped
fresh ginger

2 teaspoons garam masala

2 teaspoons ground turmeric

1/2 teaspoon chilli powder

1 teaspoon salt

1/2 cup (125ml) lemon juice

Combine fish with Masala Marinade in
large bowl, cover; stand 30 minutes.
Heat ghee in grill pan; cook fish until
browned both sides and tender.
Serve fish on a bed of baby spinach
leaves with lime wedges and
chapatis, if desired.
Masala Marinade Blend or process
ingredients until smooth.

SERVES 4
Per serving 14.7g fat; 1474kJ

38 prawn and
snake-bean curry

1.5kg medium uncooked prawns

600g snake beans

1 tablespoon peanut oil

1 large brown onion (200g), chopped finely

2 cloves garlic, crushed

1 tablespoon grated fresh ginger

2 red thai chillies, chopped finely

2 teaspoons mild curry powder

1/2 teaspoon ground turmeric

2 x 400ml cans light coconut milk

Shell and devein prawns, leaving tails intact. Cut beans into 5cm pieces. **Heat** oil in large frying pan; cook onion, garlic, ginger and chilli, stirring, until onion is soft. Stir in curry powder and turmeric; cook, stirring, until fragrant. Stir in coconut milk; simmer, uncovered, about 10 minutes or until sauce is thickened slightly.
Add beans; simmer, uncovered, 5 minutes or until tender. Add prawns; cook, stirring occasionally, until prawns have just changed in colour.

SERVES 4
Per serving 16.4g fat; 1631kJ

1 cup (150g)
raw cashews

2 teaspoons
garam masala

2 teaspoons
ground coriander

³/₄ teaspoon
chilli powder

3 cloves garlic,
chopped coarsely

2 teaspoons grated
fresh ginger

2 tablespoons
white vinegar

¹/₃ cup (80g)
tomato paste

¹/₂ cup (140g) yogurt

1kg chicken thigh
fillets, halved

80g butter

1 large brown onion
(200g), chopped finely

1 cinnamon stick

4 cardamom
pods, bruised

1 teaspoon
sweet paprika

400g can tomato puree

³/₄ cup (180ml)
chicken stock

1 cup (250ml) cream

Stir nuts, garam masala, coriander and chilli in a heated small frying pan until nuts are browned lightly. Blend or process nut mixture with garlic, ginger, vinegar, paste and half of the yogurt until just smooth. In large bowl, combine nut mixture, remaining yogurt and chicken; cover, refrigerate 3 hours or overnight.

Melt butter in large saucepan; cook onion, cinnamon and cardamom, stirring, until onion is browned. Add chicken mixture; cook, uncovered, 10 minutes. Add paprika, puree and stock, bring to a boil; reduce heat, simmer, uncovered, 45 minutes, stirring occasionally.

Remove and discard cinnamon and cardamom. Add cream; simmer, uncovered, 5 minutes.

SERVES 4
Per serving 82.2g fat; 4428kJ

40 prawns with chilli and

mustard seeds

1.5kg medium uncooked prawns

*1 large brown onion (200g),
chopped coarsely*

2 cloves garlic, chopped coarsely

*2 teaspoons coarsely chopped
fresh ginger*

2 red thai chillies, chopped coarsely

1 teaspoon ground turmeric

2 tablespoons lemon juice

2 tablespoons ghee

1 tablespoon black mustard seeds

1 teaspoon cumin seeds

1/3 cup (80ml) coconut milk

Shell and devein prawns, leaving
tails intact.
Blend or process onion, garlic, ginger,
chilli, turmeric and juice until smooth.
Heat ghee in wok or large frying pan;
stir-fry onion mixture about 5 minutes or
until browned lightly. Add seeds; stir-fry
until fragrant. Add prawns; stir-fry until
prawns have just changed in colour.
Add coconut milk; stir-fry until hot.

SERVES 4
Per serving 14.6g fat; 1320kJ

42 pork, kumara

and lentil curry

750g whole piece
pork neck

1 tablespoon
vegetable oil

2 medium brown
onions (300g),
sliced thinly

$1/4$ cup (65g) mild
curry paste

2 x 400g cans
tomatoes

1 large kumara (500g),
chopped coarsely

$1/2$ cup (100g)
red lentils

1 cup (250ml)
coconut milk

500g spinach, trimmed

1 tablespoon finely
chopped fresh
coriander leaves

Cut pork into 2cm pieces. Heat oil in large
saucepan; cook pork, in batches, until well
browned. Cook onion and paste in same pan,
stirring, until onion is soft.
Return pork to pan with undrained crushed
tomatoes, bring to a boil; reduce heat,
simmer, covered, 1$1/4$ hours.
Cook kumara, uncovered, in medium heated
oiled frying pan until just browned; add to pan
with pork mixture, stir in lentils. Bring to a boil;
reduce heat, simmer, uncovered, stirring
occasionally, about 15 minutes or until
kumara, lentils and pork are tender.
Stir in milk, spinach and coriander; cook,
stirring, until spinach is just wilted.

SERVES 4
Per serving 31g fat; 2779kJ

quick and easy
fish korma

600g thick white
fish fillets

1 tablespoon ghee

1 large brown
onion (200g),
chopped finely

1/4 cup (65g)
korma paste

1/2 cup (140g) yogurt

1 cup (250ml)
chicken stock

1 small kumara
(250g), sliced thickly

250g asparagus,
halved

1 tablespoon fresh
coriander leaves

Cut fish into 4cm pieces. Heat ghee in large non-stick frying pan; cook fish
until browned on one side, drain on absorbent paper. Cook onion and paste
in same pan, stirring, until onion is soft. Add yogurt gradually, in batches,
stirring well between additions. Add stock and kumara, bring to a boil;
reduce heat, simmer, uncovered, 15 minutes or until kumara is just tender.
Add fish and asparagus; simmer, covered, about 5 minutes or until
fish is changed in colour and vegetables are tender. Serve sprinkled
with coriander.

SERVES 4
Per serving 14.2g fat; 1420kJ

44 mild chicken

curry with lentils

1 tablespoon ghee

1 medium brown onion (150g), chopped finely

2 tablespoons mild curry paste

750g chicken thigh fillets, chopped coarsely

2 cups (500ml) chicken stock

4 curry leaves, torn

1/2 cup (100g) red lentils

1 small kumara (250g), chopped coarsely

1 cup (250ml) coconut milk

200g green beans, halved

2 tablespoons lemon juice

2 tablespoons finely chopped
fresh coriander leaves

Heat ghee in large saucepan; cook onion, stirring, until soft. Add paste and chicken; cook, stirring, until fragrant. Add stock and curry leaves, bring to a boil; reduce heat, simmer, covered, 30 minutes.
Add lentils and kumara; simmer, uncovered, about 15 minutes or until lentils and kumara are tender. Add coconut milk, beans and juice; simmer, uncovered, until beans are just tender. Stir in coriander.
Serve with steamed rice and naan, if desired.

SERVES 4
Per serving 35.6g fat; 2548kJ

46 beef madras

1 cup (90g) coarsely grated fresh coconut

400g can tomatoes

2 tablespoons grated fresh ginger

2 teaspoons black mustard seeds

1 tablespoon tamarind concentrate

2 tablespoons vegetable oil

2 large brown onions (400g), sliced thinly

6 cloves garlic, crushed

1 tablespoon ground cumin

1 teaspoon ground turmeric

2 teaspoons ground coriander

2 teaspoons chilli powder

2 teaspoons sweet paprika

10 curry leaves

1kg diced beef chuck steak

1/2 cup (125ml) water

Blend or process coconut, undrained tomatoes, ginger, seeds and tamarind until pureed. Heat oil in large saucepan; cook onion and garlic, stirring, until browned lightly. Add ground spices; cook, stirring, until fragrant.
Add curry leaves, beef, the water and coconut mixture; simmer, covered, stirring occasionally, about 1 1/2 hours or until beef is tender.

SERVES 4
Per serving 28.8g fat; 2301kJ

beef curry with coconut and almonds

1kg beef chuck steak

1 1/2 tablespoons vegetable oil

1 large brown onion (200g), sliced thinly

2 cloves garlic, crushed

1 red thai chilli, chopped finely

1/2 teaspoon ground turmeric

1 teaspoon ground coriander

1/2 teaspoon garam masala

1/4 teaspoon ground black pepper

1 teaspoon ground ginger

2 cardamom pods, bruised

1 star anise

4 curry leaves

200ml coconut milk

1/2 cup (125ml) beef stock

1/3 cup (40g) almond meal

Cut beef into 3cm pieces. Heat oil in medium saucepan; cook beef, in batches, until well browned. Cook onion and garlic in same pan, stirring, until onion is soft. Add chilli, ground spices, cardamom and star anise; cook, stirring, until fragrant. Return beef to pan with curry leaves, coconut milk and stock; simmer, covered, about 1 1/2 hours or until beef is tender. Remove cover; simmer about 15 minutes or until sauce thickens, stir in almond meal.

SERVES 4
Per serving 35g fat; 2363kJ

48 vegetable korma

1 tablespoon
vegetable oil

2 medium brown onions
(300g), chopped coarsely

2 cloves garlic, crushed

1 tablespoon black
mustard seeds

2 teaspoons cumin seeds

1/2 teaspoon
ground turmeric

1 tablespoon
ground coriander

1/2 teaspoon
ground cinnamon

2 large kumara (1kg),
chopped coarsely

2 cups (500ml)
vegetable stock

400g can tomatoes

2 tablespoons
tomato paste

11/2 cups (375ml)
coconut milk

500g cauliflower,
cut into florets

200g green
beans, halved

2 x 300g cans chickpeas,
rinsed, drained

1/4 cup coarsely chopped
fresh coriander leaves

Heat oil in large saucepan; cook onion and garlic, stirring, until onion is soft. Add seeds and ground spices; cook, stirring, until fragrant.

Add kumara; cook, stirring, 5 minutes. Add stock, undrained crushed tomatoes and paste; bring to a boil. Reduce heat; simmer, uncovered, about 15 minutes or until kumara is almost tender.

Stir in coconut milk and cauliflower; simmer, uncovered, 5 minutes. Add beans and chickpeas; simmer, uncovered, about 10 minutes or until vegetables are tender. Just before serving, stir in coriander.

SERVES 8
Per serving 14g fat; 1206kJ

50 lemon and saffron rice

1 litre (4 cups)
chicken stock

1/4 teaspoon
saffron threads

2 tablespoons ghee

2 small brown onions
(160g), sliced

2 cloves garlic,
crushed

1 teaspoon grated
fresh ginger

6 curry leaves, torn

2 teaspoons finely
grated lemon rind

2 cups (400g) basmati
rice, washed, drained

1/4 cup (60ml)
lemon juice

1/4 cup finely chopped
fresh coriander leaves

Bring stock to a boil in medium saucepan, remove from heat,
stir in saffron; cover, stand 15 minutes.
Heat ghee in medium saucepan; cook onion, garlic, ginger and curry
leaves, stirring, until onion is soft. Stir in rind. Add rice; cook, stirring,
1 minute. Stir in stock, bring to a boil; reduce heat, simmer, covered,
20 minutes or until rice is just tender and all the liquid has been absorbed.
Remove from heat, stir in juice and coriander; stand, covered, 5 minutes.

SERVES 4
Per serving 6.1g fat; 1812kJ

mixed dhal

½ cup (100g) yellow split peas

½ cup (100g) red lentils

½ cup (100g) split mung beans

2 tablespoons ghee

3 teaspoons black mustard seeds

½ teaspoon black onion seeds

2 medium brown onions (300g), chopped finely

4 cloves garlic, crushed

1 tablespoon grated fresh ginger

1 tablespoon ground cumin

3 teaspoons ground coriander

1 teaspoon ground turmeric

1 teaspoon chilli powder

2 x 400g cans tomatoes

2½ cups (625ml) vegetable stock

½ teaspoon cracked black pepper

⅓ cup (80ml) cream

2 tablespoons finely chopped fresh coriander leaves

Rinse peas, lentils and beans, separately, under cold water; drain. Place yellow split peas in small bowl, cover with water; stand for 30 minutes, drain.

Heat ghee in large heavy-base saucepan; cook seeds, stirring, until they start to pop. Add onion, garlic and ginger; cook, stirring, until onion is browned lightly.

Add ground spices; cook, stirring, for 1 minute. Add split peas, lentils, beans, undrained crushed tomatoes and stock; simmer, covered, about 30 minutes or until red lentils are tender.

Just before serving, add remaining ingredients; stir over low heat until just heated through.

SERVES 4
Per serving 22.7g fat; 1975kJ

52 vegetable
pakoras

¾ cup (110g) chickpea flour

¼ cup (35g) self-raising flour

2 teaspoons ground cumin

1 teaspoon garam masala

½ teaspoon chilli powder

¼ teaspoon ground turmeric

1 teaspoon salt

2 cloves garlic, crushed

¾ cup (180ml) water,
approximately

1 cup (85g) broccoli florets

1 cup (100g) cauliflower florets

vegetable oil, for deep-frying

1 small eggplant (230g),
sliced thinly

2 medium zucchini (240g),
sliced thinly

yogurt mint dipping sauce

2 tablespoons bottled
mint jelly

¾ cup (210g) yogurt

1 red thai chilli,
chopped finely

Sift flours, spices and salt into medium bowl. Add garlic, whisk in enough water to make a thick batter. Cover, refrigerate 30 minutes.

Boil, steam or microwave broccoli and cauliflower, separately, until just tender. Rinse under cold water, pat dry with absorbent paper.

Heat oil in large saucepan. Dip vegetables pieces, one at a time, into batter, drain away excess. Deep-fry vegetables, in batches, in hot oil, until browned lightly and crisp.

Drain on absorbent paper. Serve with Yogurt Mint Dipping Sauce.

Yogurt Mint Dipping Sauce Combine ingredients in small bowl; cover, refrigerate at least 1 hour.

SERVES 4
Per serving 11g fat; 1086kJ

54 cardamom spiced pilaf with pistachios

2 tablespoons ghee

2 teaspoons cardamom seeds

1 medium brown onion (150g),
chopped finely

1 clove garlic, crushed

1 teaspoon grated fresh ginger

2 curry leaves, torn

1 red thai chilli, chopped finely

2 cups (400g) basmati rice, washed, drained

1 litre (4 cups) chicken stock

1/2 cup (75g) shelled pistachios

2 tablespoons finely chopped
fresh mint leaves

Heat ghee in medium saucepan; cook
seeds, stirring, until they begin to pop.
Add onion; cook, stirring, until onion is
soft. Add garlic, ginger, curry leaves and
chilli; cook, stirring, until fragrant.
Add rice; cook, stirring, 1 minute. Add stock,
bring to a boil; reduce heat, simmer, covered
tightly, about 20 minutes or until rice is just
tender and all the liquid has been absorbed.
Remove from heat, fluff rice with a fork,
stir in pistachios and mint; stand,
covered, 5 minutes.

SERVES 4
Per serving 20g fat; 2437kJ

56 chapatis

1 cup (150g) white plain flour
1 cup (160g) wholemeal plain flour
1 teaspoon salt
1 tablespoon ghee
³⁄₄ cup (180ml) warm water, approximately

Place flours and salt into large bowl, rub in ghee. Add enough water to mix to a firm dough. Knead dough on floured surface for 10 minutes, working in about an extra ¹⁄₄ cup (35g) plain white flour. Cover dough with cloth, stand 1 hour.

Divide dough into 14 portions. Roll each piece, on floured surface, into a 20cm round, cover with a cloth, stand 10 minutes before cooking.

Heat grill plate or heavy-base frying pan until very hot; cook one round at a time, for about 30 seconds on first side or until round just begins to colour; remove from pan. Place uncooked side of chapati directly over medium flame, checking frequently until chapati begins to blister. Repeat with remaining rounds. Wrap cooked chapatis in a cloth to keep warm while cooking remainder.

MAKES 14
Per serving 1.6g fat; 354kJ

front: rotis
back: chapatis

rotis 57

1 cup (150g) white plain flour
1 cup (160g) wholemeal plain flour
1 teaspoon salt
1 teaspoon ground coriander
½ teaspoon ground turmeric
2 teaspoons cumin seeds
1 tablespoon vegetable oil
¾ cup (180ml) water, approximately
90g ghee, approximately

Sift flours, salt and ground spices into large bowl. Make a well in flour, add seeds, oil and enough water to mix to a soft dough. Knead dough on floured surface for 10 minutes. Wrap dough in plastic, refrigerate 30 minutes.
Divide dough into 16 portions, roll each piece, on floured surface, into a 16cm round. Heat heavy-base frying pan until very hot, add about 1 teaspoon of the ghee, quickly turn pan to coat base with ghee. Place roti into pan; cook about 1 minute or until roti is puffed slightly and bubbles begin to form. Turn roti, brown other side. Repeat with remaining ghee and dough. When ghee begins to burn in pan and a few roti have been cooked, wipe pan clean with absorbent paper.

MAKES 16
Per serving 7.2g fat; 527kJ

58 naan

²/₃ cup (160ml) warm water

1 teaspoon dry yeast

1 teaspoon sugar

2 cups (300g) plain flour

1 teaspoon salt

80g ghee, melted

2 tablespoons yogurt

2 teaspoons black onion seeds

Whisk the water, yeast and sugar in small bowl until yeast is dissolved; cover, stand in warm place 10 minutes. Place flour and salt into large bowl; add yeast mixture, half the ghee and yogurt. Mix to a soft dough then knead, on floured surface, about 5 minutes or until dough is smooth and elastic.

Place dough in large oiled bowl; cover, stand in warm place for about 1½ hours or until the dough is doubled in size.

Knead dough on floured surface for 5 minutes. Divide dough into six portions, roll each piece into a 20cm round.

Cover oven tray with foil; grease foil. Cook naan, one at a time, under very hot grill for about 2 minutes each side or until puffed and just browned. Brush naan with a little of the remaining ghee, sprinkle with some of the seeds; grill for a further 30 seconds. Wrap cooked naan in a cloth to keep warm while cooking remainder.

MAKES 6
Per serving 12.5g fat; 1200kJ

parathas

1 cup (160g) wholemeal plain flour

1 cup (150g) white plain flour

1/2 teaspoon salt

100g ghee, chopped coarsely

1/2 cup (125ml) water, approximately

100g ghee, extra

filling

1 large potato (300g), chopped coarsely

1/2 small kumara (125g), chopped coarsely

1 teaspoon coriander seeds, bruised

1/2 teaspoon ground cumin

1/4 teaspoon cayenne pepper

1/4 cup firmly packed fresh coriander leaves

Place flours and salt into large bowl, rub in ghee. Stir in enough water to bind ingredients. Knead dough on floured surface 10 minutes or until dough is smooth.
Divide dough into 16 portions; on floured surface, roll each piece into a 16cm round. Stack rounds between layers of plastic wrap to prevent drying out. Divide Filling among eight rounds. Spread Filling over rounds, leaving 7mm borders. Brush borders with water, top with remaining rounds, press edges together to seal.
Heat some of the extra ghee in large frying pan; cook parathas, in batches, until browned and slightly puffed on both sides; drain on absorbent paper. Repeat with remaining ghee and parathas.
Filling Boil, steam or microwave potato and kumara until tender. Mash vegetables coarsely in medium bowl, stir in remaining ingredients.

MAKES 8
Per serving 25.8g fat; 1616kJ

glossary

almond meal also known as finely ground almonds; almonds ground to a flour-like texture.

basmati rice see Indian Essential Ingredients (page 3).

beef
blade steak: from the shoulder blade area.
chuck steak: from the neck area.

butter beans small white beans also known as cannellini beans.

cardamom see Indian Essential Ingredients (page 2).

chickpeas also called garbanzos or channa; a round, sandy-coloured legume.

coconut
cream: see Indian Essential Ingredients (page 3).
flaked: dried, flaked coconut flesh.
grated fresh: can be from a whole fresh coconut or bought, frozen, in packets.
light milk: available in cans and cartons.
milk: see Indian Essential Ingredients (page 3).

milk powder: dehydrated powdered coconut milk.

coriander also known as cilantro or Chinese parsley; leafy bright-green herb best added just before dish is to be served, for maximum impact.

cream also known as pure cream and pouring cream.
sour: a thick, commercially cultured soured cream.

curry
korma paste: a mild paste.
paste (mild): made from oil, tomato puree, coriander, cumin and chickpea flour.
powder (mild): spice blend; can consist of dried chilli, cinnamon, coriander, mace, fenugreek, cumin, fennel, cardamom and turmeric.
tikka paste: based on lentil flour, oil, garlic, ginger and a variety of spices.
vindaloo paste: a fiery hot/sour paste based on tamarind, lentil flour, ginger, garlic and spices.

eggplant also known as aubergine.

fenugreek seeds small, mustard-brown, flat seeds having a sharp, bitter flavour.

flour
chickpea: made from ground chickpeas; also known as garam flour or besan.
plain: all-purpose wheat flour.
self-raising: plain flour sifted with baking powder in the proportion of 1 cup flour to 2 teaspoons baking powder.
wholemeal: all-purpose wholewheat flour.

garam masala see Indian Essential Ingredients (page 2).

ghee see Indian Essential Ingredients (page 3).

ginger see Indian Essential Ingredients (page 3).

hot lime pickle available bottled from supermarkets.

kumara orange-fleshed sweet potato.

lamb
fillet: tenderloin.
minced: ground lamb.
mini lamb roasts (trim lamb round or topside): comes from the chump and leg, eye of loin and loin.

mustard seeds, black
see Indian Essential
Ingredients (page 3).

mustard seeds, yellow
the seed of a plant from
the cabbage family; have
mild, nutty flavour.

oil
peanut: pressed from
ground peanuts.
vegetable: oil sourced
from a variety of plants,
not animal fats.

onion
black onion seeds: also
known as kalonji
or nigella.
green: also known as
scallion or (incorrectly)
shallot; an immature
onion with long, bright-
green edible stalk.
red: also known as
Spanish, red Spanish or
Bermuda onion; sweet
purple-red onion.

pappadums sun-dried
wafers made of flour,
oil and spice.

prawns also known
as shrimp.

saffron available in strands
or ground; imparts yellow
colour once infused.

sambal oelek (also ulek or
olek) salty chilli paste.

sesame seeds black and
white oval seeds harvested
from a tropical plant.

spinach also known as
English spinach and
(incorrectly) silverbeet;
has delicate green leaves
on thin stems. Good served
raw in salads.

split mung beans
also known as split
moong beans.

star anise dried star-
shaped pod; seeds taste
of aniseed.

stock 1 cup stock is the
equivalent of 1 cup water
plus 1 crumbled stock
cube or 1 teaspoon
stock powder.

sugar we used coarse,
granulated table sugar,
unless otherwise specified.
brown: soft, fine granulated
sugar retaining molasses.
palm: also known as gula
jawa or melaka, or jaggery;
fine coconut palm sugar.

sultanas golden raisins.

tamarind
concentrate: a thick,
purple-black, ready-to-
use paste.
dried: to extract essence,
soak in boiling water
until cool then press
through sieve back into
the water; discard pulp,
use flavoured water.

tandoori powder
flavourless mixture of
yellow- and red-coloured
powdered vegetable dye.

yeast a 7g (¼ oz) sachet
of dried yeast is equal
to 15g (½ oz) of
compressed yeast.

yellow split peas also known
as field peas; a legume.

yogurt we used unflavoured,
full-fat cow milk yogurt.

zucchini also known
as courgette.

62 index

facts and figures 63

These conversions are approximate only, but the difference between an exact and the approximate conversion of various liquid and dry measures is minimal and will not affect your cooking results.

Note: NZ, Canada, US and UK all use 15ml tablespoons. Australian tablespoons measure 20ml. All cup and spoon measurements are level.

Measuring equipment

The difference between one country's measuring cups and another's is, at most, within a 2 or 3 teaspoon variance. (For the record, 1 Australian metric measuring cup holds approximately 250ml.) The most accurate way of measuring dry ingredients is to weigh them. For liquids, use a clear glass or plastic jug having metric markings.

How to measure

When using graduated measuring cups, shake dry ingredients loosely into the appropriate cup. Do not tap the cup on a bench or tightly pack the ingredients unless directed to do so. Level the top of measuring cups and measuring spoons with a knife. When measuring liquids, place a clear glass or plastic jug having metric markings on a flat surface to check accuracy at eye level.

Dry measures

metric	imperial
15g	½oz
30g	1oz
60g	2oz
90g	3oz
125g	4oz (¼lb)
155g	5oz
185g	6oz
220g	7oz
250g	8oz (½lb)
280g	9oz
315g	10oz
345g	11oz
375g	12oz (¾lb)
410g	13oz
440g	14oz
470g	15oz
500g	16oz (1lb)
750g	24oz (1½lb)
1kg	32oz (2lb)

We use large eggs with an average weight of 60g.

Liquid measures

metric	imperial
30 ml	1 fluid oz
60 ml	2 fluid oz
100 ml	3 fluid oz
125 ml	4 fluid oz
150 ml	5 fluid oz (¼ pint/1 gill)
190 ml	6 fluid oz
250 ml (1cup)	8 fluid oz
300 ml	10 fluid oz (½ pint)
500 ml	16 fluid oz
600 ml	20 fluid oz (1 pint)
1000 ml (1litre)	1¾ pints

Helpful measures

metric	imperial
3mm	⅛in
6mm	¼in
1cm	½in
2cm	¾in
2.5cm	1in
6cm	2½in
8cm	3in
20cm	8in
23cm	9in
25cm	10in
30cm	12in (1ft)

Oven temperatures

These oven temperatures are only a guide for conventional ovens. For fan-forced ovens, check the manufacturer's manual.

	°C (Celsius)	°F (Fahrenheit)	Gas Mark
Very slow	120	250	½
Slow	150	275 – 300	1 – 2
Moderately slow	160	325	3
Moderate	180	350 – 375	4 – 5
Moderately hot	200	400	6
Hot	220	425 – 450	7 – 8
Very hot	240	475	9

ARE YOU MISSING SOME OF THE WORLD'S FAVOURITE COOKBOOKS?

The Australian Women's Weekly cookbooks are available from bookshops, cookshops, supermarkets and other stores all over the world. You can also buy direct from the publisher, using the order form below.

Mini Series £2.50 190x138mm 64 pages			
	QTY		QTY
4 Fast Ingredients		Italian	
15-minute Feasts		Jams & Jellies	
30-minute Meals		Kids Party Food	
50 Fast Chicken Fillets		Last-minute Meals	
After-work Stir-fries		Lebanese Cooking	
Barbecue		Malaysian Favourites	
Barbecue Chicken		Microwave	
Barbecued Seafood		Mince	
Biscuits, Brownies & Biscotti		Muffins	
Bites		Noodles	
Bowl Food		Party Food	
Burgers, Rösti & Fritters		Pasta	
Cafe Cakes		Pickles and Chutneys	
Cafe Food		Potatoes	
Casseroles		Risotto	
Char-grills & Barbecues		Roast	
Cheesecakes, Pavlovas & Trifles		Salads	
Chocolate		Seafood	
Chocolate Cakes		Simple Slices	
Christmas Cakes & Puddings		Simply Seafood	
Cocktails		Skinny Food	
Curries		Stir-fries	
Drinks		Summer Salads	
Fast Fish		Tapas, Antipasto & Mezze	
Fast Food for Friends		Thai Cooking	
Fast Soup		Thai Favourites	
Finger Food		Vegetarian	
From the Shelf		Vegetarian Stir-fries	
Gluten-free Cooking		Vegie Main Meals	
Ice-creams & Sorbets		Wok	
Indian Cooking		**TOTAL COST**	**£**

NAME

ADDRESS

POSTCODE

DAYTIME PHONE

I ENCLOSE MY CHEQUE/MONEY ORDER FOR £

OR PLEASE CHARGE MY VISA, ACCESS OR MASTERCARD NUMBER

CARDHOLDER'S NAME

EXPIRY DATE

CARDHOLDER'S SIGNATURE

To order: Mail or fax – photocopy or complete the order form above, and send your credit card details or cheque payable to: Australian Consolidated Press (UK), Moulton Park Business Centre, Red House Road, Moulton Park, Northampton NN3 6AQ, phone (+44) (01) 604 497531, fax (+44) (01) 604 497533, e-mail books@acpuk.com. Or order online at **www.acpuk.com**
Non-UK residents: We accept the credit cards listed on the coupon, or cheques, drafts or International Money Orders payable in sterling and drawn on a UK bank. Credit card charges are at the exchange rate current at the time of payment.
Postage and packing UK: Add £1.00 per order plus 25p per book.
Postage and packing overseas: Add £2.00 per order plus 50p per book.
Offer ends 31.12.2006

Food director Pamela Clark
Food editor Karen Hammial
Assistant food editor Kathy McGarry
Assistant recipe editor Elizabeth Hooper
ACP BOOKS
Editorial director Susan Tomnay
Creative director Hieu Chi Nguyen
Senior editor Julie Collard
Concept design Jackie Richards
Designer Caryl Wiggins
Sales director Brian Cearnes
Brand manager Renée Crea
Production manager Carol Currie
Chief executive officer John Alexander
Group publisher Pat Ingram
Publisher Sue Wannan
Editorial director (AWW) Deborah Thomas
Produced by ACP Books, Sydney.
Printing by Dai Nippon Printing in Korea.
Published by ACP Publishing Pty Limited,
54 Park St, Sydney;
GPO Box 4088, Sydney, NSW 2001.
Ph: (02) 9282 8618 Fax: (02) 9267 9438.
acpbooks@acp.com.au
www.acpbooks.com.au
To order books phone 136 116.
Send recipe enquiries to
Recipeenquiries@acp.com.au
RIGHTS ENQUIRIES
Laura Bamford, Director ACP Books.
lbamford@acplon.co.uk
Ph: +44 (207) 812 6526
Australia Distributed by Network Services,
GPO Box 4088, Sydney, NSW 1028.
Ph: (02) 9282 8777 Fax: (02) 9264 3278.
United Kingdom Distributed by Australian
Consolidated Press (UK), Moulton Park Business
Centre, Red House Road, Moulton Park, Northam
NN3 6AQ. Ph: (01604) 497 531
Fax: (01604) 497 533 acpukltd@aol.com
Canada Distributed by Whitecap Books Ltd,
351 Lynn Ave, North Vancouver, BC, V7J 2C4,
Ph: (604) 980 9852 Fax: (604) 980 8197
customerservice@whitecap.ca
www.whitecap.ca
New Zealand Distributed by Netlink Distribution
Company, ACP Media Centre, Cnr Fanshawe
and Beaumont Streets, Westhaven, Auckland.
PO Box 47906, Ponsonby, Auckland, NZ.
Ph: (9) 366 9966 ask@ndc.co.nz
South Africa Distributed by PSD Promotions,
30 Diesel Road, Isando, Gauteng, Johannesburg
PO Box 1175, Isando, 1600, Gauteng, Johannest
Ph: (27 11) 392 6065/7 Fax: (27 11) 392 6079/8
orders@psdprom.co.za

Clark, Pamela.
The Australian Women's Weekly
Indian Cooking

Includes index.
ISBN 1 86396 232 8

1. Cookery, Indian.
I. Title: Australian Women's Weekly.
641.5954

© ACP Magazines Ltd 2001
ABN 18 053 273 546

First published 2001. Reprinted 2001, 2004, 200

Cover Lamb, butter bean and spinach curry, pag
Stylist Vicki Liley
Photographer Mark O'Meara
Back cover at left, Prawns with chilli and mustai
seeds, page 40; at right, Vegetable korma, page

The publishers would like to thank the following fo
props used in photography:
Acorn Trading; Country Road Homewares; Mosn
Mud Australia; Ruby Star Traders; and Shack.